LIGHTNING STRIKES TWICE

*secret confessions
of a career-woman-turned-caregiver*

LIGHTNING STRIKES TWICE

*secret confessions
of a career-woman-turned-caregiver*

essay and poems by

SONYA K. SINGH

IGUANA

Copyright © 2019 Sonya K. Singh
Published by Iguana Books
720 Bathurst Street, Suite 303
Toronto, Ontario, Canada
M5S 2R4

All rights reserved. No part of this publication may be reproduced, stored in a retrieval system or transmitted, in any form or by any means, electronic, mechanical, recording or otherwise (except brief passages for purposes of review) without the prior permission of the author or a licence from The Canadian Copyright Licensing Agency (Access Copyright). For an Access Copyright licence, visit www.accesscopyright.ca or call toll free to 1-800-893-5777.

Publisher: Meghan Behse
Editor: Lee Parpart
Front cover illustration: Marie-Judith Jean-Louis
Back cover photograph: Kristen Clancy
Cover design: Daniella Postavsky
Interior illustrations: Emily Finch

978-1-77180-306-9 (paperback).
978-1-77180-313-7 (epub).
978-1-77180-314-4 (Kindle).

This is an original print edition of *Lightning Strikes Twice*.

This book is dedicated to my loving mother and father and to the beauty that makes up my sisters.

It is also dedicated to all the caregivers around the world.

Acknowledgements

This book was made possible because of the encouragement from award-winning poet Kate Marshall Flaherty. Despite many friendships that floated away, others were resilient during these tough times. I would like to thank my best friend of 15 years, Michael Potter, for staying up on those late nights and listening to me read a few lines and never doubting my angst. A special shoutout to my bestie Colleen Murphy. Even though she's in Calgary she was always able to find time to ask me how I was doing or send me something in the mail to put a smile on my face. To fellow authors Jasmine Aziz and Dan McNeil, thank you for always, ALWAYS encouraging me to explore my creativity and to never lose my words. To Daniel Pillai for always being so proud of me and for being the first one to champion and support anything I do, and to Onelia Estudillo, who one day picked up the phone and called me to cry with me. Thank you so much for that moment. And to my sisters Tina and Rupa, for all of our moments during these times, thank you for always knowing what to do.

A special thank you to Iguana Books for believing in me and that this story could even be shared, and to my AMAZING editor, Lee Parpart. All those late nights and brilliant discussions kept me sane.

And most of all, thank you to Mom and Dad for letting me take care of you. My heart loves you much.

Introduction

When I started working on this book in 2018, I had never written a line of poetry. Like a lot of people, I read poetry in school, and at some point, I became a huge fan of Oscar Wilde. Years later, I became hooked on the spare, meme-like poetry posts of Instagram stars like Atticus and R.H. Sin. But I felt no need to write any poetry of my own.

Looking back, I can see that this was probably because my life was too busy, and in many ways too fortunate, to demand the kind of outlet that poetry can offer people in times of need.

As a 40-year-old South Asian woman living in Canada, I felt I had made it, professionally. I had worked in a series of interesting media jobs across Canada and in the United States, and I was quickly rising through the ranks as a public relations director since returning to Toronto to be closer to my family. I had good friends — scratch that, I had great friends — and a rich, busy social life. I visited my family every couple of weeks, and I worked hard at my job, earning enough money to buy a second home in downtown Toronto. To top it all off, I was finally in a relationship that was progressing in what I thought at the time was the right direction.

Then, in the space of a few months, everything changed. After decades of good health and a lot of wonderful luck as they worked to build their family and buy their own home, my parents were hit by back-to-back health crises. One would have been enough, but when both of them became ill, our family was left reeling, and my two younger sisters and I suddenly became caregivers. This book is a poetic record of how I coped with that double lightning strike.

The first crisis seemed to come on in slow motion. It was early 2017 when my father started complaining of persistent pain in his legs. I remember thinking that it was just a symptom of age, or maybe the effect of too much time spent hunched over his prized vegetables in the garden he loved so much. Surely that was all this was — a man having to adjust his routines to account for a little more stiffness as he entered his 60s. But the complaints continued, and the pain got worse. After a while, he started having trouble doing simple things like getting up off a chair and moving around the house. None of us — not me, my sisters, nor our mother — could believe that anything was seriously wrong. This was Dad, after all — the life of the party and the first to hit the dance floor (and to stay there, captivating guests with his Bollywood moves) during any family celebration. Now he was having trouble walking from the couch to his bedroom.

One weekend in 2017, after hearing Dad's complaints again, I decided to go home and investigate. I was no stranger to Dr. Google, and all my years of self-diagnosing every ache and bump in my own body would help me to get a handle on my dad's symptoms. Of course, I knew that Dr. Google could also be a source of anxiety and misinformation, but I was hoping my skills at online sleuthing would help to rule out any major conditions, while creating some kind of reassurance that my dad was all right. And he *was*. During my visit, we talked, we ate, and we laughed. He seemed *fine*. He had just taken a few spills. He was getting older, and he needed to make some adjustments to his routines. If he needed to, he could use the cane we bought him to venture out on any long walks.

Since I thought I was right, we went on with the rest of our day and got ready to head to our favourite father-daughter spot, Canadian Tire. Dad always loved Canadian Tire, and would spend hours wandering through the home-hardware aisles. I enjoyed going with him and didn't mind that he often made me pay for everything. I laughed when he always asked for some extra cash on the side, which I was never to tell Mom about.

I went to warm up the car. It was a cold, rainy day in early spring. I saw him walk out of the house with cane in hand, and as he moved toward the car, I glanced down to plug in my phone. When I looked back up, my dad wasn't walking to the car anymore. I couldn't see him, but I could see his cane lying on the front step of the house. I jumped out of the car while it was still running and ran over to find him lying face-down on the concrete ground, wincing in pain. His glasses were lying on the ground, several feet away. The lumberjack hat I had bought him for Christmas lay next to him, covered in blood from his forehead and nose. I dropped to his side and tried to reassure him. When I went to help him up, I couldn't lift him, and the rain somehow made him seem heavier. Looking back, I can see that the rain obviously had nothing to do with it. I was imagining things, because in the moment I was helping my dad up from this horrible fall, my heart was breaking, and my body was suddenly a lot weaker. When I finally pulled myself together, I found that it was easier to help him from the left side. We got up slowly. I told him it was the rain. *Dad, it was the rain. The stupid cane isn't strong enough. It slipped, and that's why you fell.* But deep down, I knew something else was wrong.

By the summer of 2017, we finally had an answer. After many rounds of testing, our father was diagnosed with progressive supranuclear palsy (PSP), a less well-known neurodegenerative brain condition, sometimes misdiagnosed as Parkinson's disease, that affects about 20,000 Americans. There is no known cause and no cure. There is just pain. Pain that affects walking, swallowing, mood, and balance, which explained why my dad was falling.

I had a difficult time with this news. My mind went into "save mode" for several months. I called in favours at private healthcare facilities, looking for a cure, and at one point my credit card statement read like an index of infomercial products. I even bought Larry King's joint pain relief pills. After all, he was 84 and still walking and talking. Maybe he knew something that the doctors didn't. As one alternative remedy after another failed to produce results, I finally had to admit that the doctors hadn't missed anything. I just wasn't ready to jump into "accept mode." I did, eventually, after a small exercise bike arrived at our home, promising that in only 15 minutes a day, my dad would be walking on his own again. Three months after my dad was diagnosed, he never regained his mobility. The bike broke its promise.

My sisters and I were just beginning to cope with this terrible new reality when the other lightning bolt hit. A few months after our father's diagnosis, our mother became the next victim of what began to feel like a family curse. After working herself ragged caring for our dad while his health deteriorated, she suffered an accident that left her unable to care for our father and in need of a caregiver of her own.

To help you understand how this affected our family, I need to tell you a bit about my mother. Compared with our dad, she was a lot less flamboyant. As quiet as she was, though, her beauty was loud. My father used to tell us that of all the women he could have chosen (their marriage was arranged), he picked the tallest and the most beautiful one. Of course, it didn't hurt that she was seven years younger than our dad when she married him at age 19. Despite the age difference between them, our mom always seemed to hold her own. At five-foot-eight, she commanded the attention of any room she entered. Her face was always carefully made up, and there was nothing subtle about her choice of makeup. From the bright pink on her sculpted cheekbones to her bold red Avon lips, her shyness attracted even more attention to her than if she had been outgoing or more confident. She was refined and reminded me of Indian royalty. She hopped on a plane with only a few words of English picked up from the local cable station in her Indian city and uprooted her life to be with a husband who was chosen for her. She didn't choose the life she later ended up having, with a husband and three daughters, but she chose a life that allowed my two younger sisters and me to make choices. Our mother worked long hours, plus overtime, doing piecework in a factory for more than 25 years, to give us that freedom.

One day in 2017, when she was running a bunch of errands for our father, she let herself get dehydrated, but she kept going, and started to make lunch for the two of them. As she lifted the top off a slow cooker full of hot lentils, the steam hit her in the face and sent her reeling backwards in a dead faint. As she fell, her arm caught the handle and dragged the large slow cooker on top of her, emptying its entire contents onto her unconscious body. The superheated lentils stayed there on her skin while our father heard noises from the kitchen and struggled to get up from the living room couch to come to her aid. When he finally succeeded in alerting a neighbour who called an ambulance, our mother was transported to the hospital. This accident left her with burns to 44 percent of her body, including third-degree burns and nerve damage that resulted in a two-month hospital stay and multiple surgeries.

To say that my sisters and I were devastated doesn't quite capture it. I felt broken, and suffered overwhelming guilt for not being there when her accident happened. That guilt was pushed to the side as weekly visits turned into two months of constant driving: an hour every day to see my mother at the hospital, then another 45 minutes home to see my dad, followed by another hour-and-a-half to get back to my home in Toronto. Every day my dad would ask how our mom was, and every day we knew he couldn't go to the hospital. Her condition was too severe and his mobility was too restricted to make it smart for him to visit. My dad couldn't remember much from the day the tragic events unfolded. He was still in shock, so we only told him what we felt he could handle. There was no way for his brain to process the event, especially with his disease progressing rapidly.

As the days wore on, I was on autopilot. Most days I couldn't remember the drive to the burn unit. I slept on chairs at the hospital, and the lack of sleep left me delirious. My sisters and I were all being run ragged trying to juggle work, visiting our mom, taking care of our dad, and taking care of each other. I hadn't seen my friends in weeks, and a reminder here or there would come in through text, but none of my friends came to visit my mother or me. After a while, my disappointment turned to numbness, as the only emotions I had were dedicated to my family. I didn't have time to argue with close friends about why I needed them or why I felt they should be there for me. The same laser focus on my family would also start to spell the end of my relationship with my boyfriend. We went from talking about marriage and kids to splitting up when he accused me of having no time or energy left for him. Looking back, he was right. Every shred of energy and attention I had to give was going into caring for my parents.

Two months passed, and it was finally time to bring Mom home. At this point, my sisters and I had new decisions to make about our parents' care. We knew from the outset that they would want to stay in their own home. After emigrating to Canada from India in their late teens, our mom and dad had both worked hard in factory jobs. Everything they had earned either went to raise my sisters and me, helped pay for their home in Guelph, Ontario, or ended up in a modest retirement fund that was intended to realize their dream of travelling across India and visiting as many temples as they could. They were not about to give up the house they had designed themselves and worked so hard to build. They also wanted to be together. Despite having an arranged marriage, over four decades they had become inseparable and were still very much in love. Above all, they did *not* want to leave this world in separate hospitals. This meant that my sisters and I needed to become caregivers in their house.

After a few months of trying to manage the situation while travelling for work and living in my new home in Toronto, I was worn down, and feeling as though I was not offering enough support to my sisters. Both of them had stepped up in a big way, and I needed to do the same. I was scrambling every day at work and increasingly unable to focus. Overwhelmed by the task of juggling work and the needs of my family, I finally surrendered to the new reality, listed my house on Airbnb, and moved back home to become a full-time caregiver to my parents.

This decision was swift and I didn't consult anyone, not even the man I was dating. He woke up one day to find my bags packed and me loading my car with personal belongings to take back to Guelph. He was puzzled. After all, he thought we would be spending the summer living together and hosting friends for backyard barbeques. When I look back at my decision, I realize that I had checked out of the relationship months earlier, at around the time of my father's diagnosis. The same hard truth also applies to my friendships. Less than a handful of my closest friends knew the full story of what was going on with my parents, and even fewer knew that I was moving back home. It would seem silly to not share this with close friends and the people that I loved the most, but I realize now that I was trying to manage the situation by limiting how much I told people. The more I contained the news, the less real my parents' illnesses felt. Subconsciously, I must have believed that the more people knew, the sicker my mom and dad really were.

As soon as I moved home and became a full-time caregiver to my parents, reality came crashing in. Everything in my life changed. I went from picking out curtains and furniture for my new house in downtown Toronto to sleeping in my childhood bedroom again, surrounded by pictures and tchotchkes from high school. Instead of running daily PR meetings at work, I spent my days running around town picking up prescriptions and medical supplies. I drove my parents to all of their appointments and I listened to the doctors explain their symptoms and treatment, when treatment was available. I cleaned the house, and I interviewed caregivers who could give me a few hours of relief now and then. I also cooked all of my parents' meals, in part because my mom had nerve damage to both hands, and in part because she could no longer be in the kitchen, where she'd suffered a trauma. I was slowly moving into a place referred to as "caregiver burnout."

Whenever I had time, I scoured the internet looking for ways to give my parents relief. I spent thousands of dollars on contraptions that promised to help my father walk again, and on second opinions from online physicians, before I finally realized that there were no easy answers — that I could not buy or invent a miracle cure that would put everything right and return all of our lives to normal. With my hopes dashed, I re-dedicated myself to giving my parents the best care possible, and to keeping them as comfortable as they could be. Meanwhile, old boundaries and privacies were shattered as I settled into my new role as a full-time caregiver, helping my mom and dad with every aspect of their daily lives, from eating and getting dressed to going to the bathroom.

I had joined the ranks of millions of caregivers who are caring for elderly or ill family members worldwide, and it was giving me a lot of...*feelings*.

One of the ways I coped was by writing. I couldn't sleep, because I never knew when one or both of my parents would need help, and I was terrified of missing a medical emergency. Writing became an important outlet for the daily storms of emotion that came with the transition to full-time caregiving. I would retreat to my room after my parents finally went to sleep and turn to my notebooks for solace. I began hurling my thoughts and feelings onto the page with the kind of energy that most people reserve for diaries written in their teens. I tried writing a memoir of what was happening, going back to my childhood to explore my family life before my father's illness and my mother's accident. But when it came down to it, I needed poetry to help me through the worst of the crisis. Poetry satisfied two main requirements: It fit into my hectic life, since it could be done in short bursts, and it allowed me to vent feelings that I found difficult to express in any other form. Something about the direct emotional pathways offered by poetry helped me work through the pain of watching my parents suffer and of seeing my own life, and many of my old friendships, float away.

The poems that make up this collection are not always wise, balanced, or uplifting. This book is a raw cry from the heart about what it's like to suddenly lose your independence and watch yourself become an orphan in slow motion.

The emotions that I deal with in these poems are not all pretty, in part because I no longer felt pretty. Gone were the days of curling my hair and putting on makeup. I had traded those rituals for occasional showers and early-onset alopecia (an autoimmune condition that results in hair loss and spot baldness). In a pattern that will be familiar to caregivers around the world, I struggled to care for myself because all of my care was dedicated to my loving parents. Some of these poems feel like dirges to a lost self. Others read like the bratty expressions of a new caregiver who just wants to go out on the town with her friends again, or enjoy the simple pleasure (not to mention the necessity) of earning a paycheque. Other poems rail at the selfishness of relatives who send food over to the house or call on the phone while avoiding the harder work of visiting in person. Some of the most private and difficult poems in this book speak to tensions in my own family, as my sisters and I have struggled to agree on how to care for our parents. While we may have fought sometimes, we know that it's because we're afraid of losing our mom and dad, and that our fear has sometimes led to anger. These poems speak to the complexity of our different responses to this impending loss.

When I look back on these poems now (with less than a year of hindsight in most cases), I can already see that these were the cries of a person struggling to adjust to a challenging new role in life. They are also poems of, and about, hope. One thing I've come to believe as a result of this journey is that no one should try to take away a caregiver's hope, no matter how fragile or even misguided that hope might seem. Caregivers need to be allowed to work through the stages of denial and acceptance at our own pace. There are times when we just want to hang onto the fragile belief that our loved one will live longer than expected, or that maybe, just maybe, we'll be the ones to beat the odds. No one should try to rush this process or push caregivers into a state of acceptance. Sometimes we just need to nurse the hope that everything will be fine — even when it seems obvious to everyone else that it may not be.

Full disclosure: There is some pretty intense anger in this book. I could have edited the anger out. That might have made me look better. But I wasn't about to paper over the rough parts of the caregiving process. Giving up your life to care for someone you love, while watching them decline mentally and/or physically, is painful and at times enraging. It pushes every button most of us have, and creates new ones. I wanted to make space for all of the feelings that go along with caregiving, from the most negative to the most positive, including the moments of laughter that I have shared with my parents on this journey. It has been a privilege like no other to care for my loving parents, and I hope that's made clear in these pages. But in describing that privilege, I didn't want to spread the myth that caregiving is all about going from one graceful epiphany to the next. Sometimes you're just tired, upset, sweaty, and out of patience, and that's okay.

These poems will not necessarily heal your troubled soul or make caregiving seem like a noble cause. But they do tell the truth — my truth, at least — about the seismic disruptions that come with giving up your old life to tend to someone else's needs.

I hope this book will say the things that some caregivers often feel pressured to keep secret. Caregivers are expected to be stoic at all times. We're supposed to be paragons of virtue and self-control who never swear or feel anger or experience self-pity. But I'm here to say that swearing and anger and self-pity are all very real aspects of being a full-time caregiver for a family member (or two, in my case) who has suddenly become incapacitated. It makes no sense to force caregivers to stuff these feelings back inside. Repression leads to depression, and as caregivers, we need to stay strong, both for ourselves and for the people who depend on us for daily comfort.

If you're a caregiver, I hope you read this book and feel "seen" and validated by the truth-telling on these pages. I hope you also feel proud of the role that you've chosen to take on, because I know that even in my darkest moments, that sense of pride never leaves me.

If you're a close friend or a family member of a caregiver, I hope you'll read this book and think about how you can be most helpful.

Spoiler alert: Put in the time! If someone you know is chronically ill or caring for a person with a chronic condition, don't just call one of them and ask how *they* are doing! Visit the person who is receiving care, and while you're there, look for ways to support the caregiver. Make sure they know how much you appreciate the time and energy they're putting into caring for your mutual loved one. Send them out for a spa day, or down the hall for a nap. Bring food, yes, but also bring your whole self, and listen — really listen — to the caregiver and the person who is receiving their daily help.

Thank you for taking the time to read this book. Writing it has been a labour of love and self-care, and I hope that it helps some of the millions of caregivers out there who have changed their lives in order to help a loved one in their time of greatest need.

Sonya K. Singh
Guelph, Ontario
2019

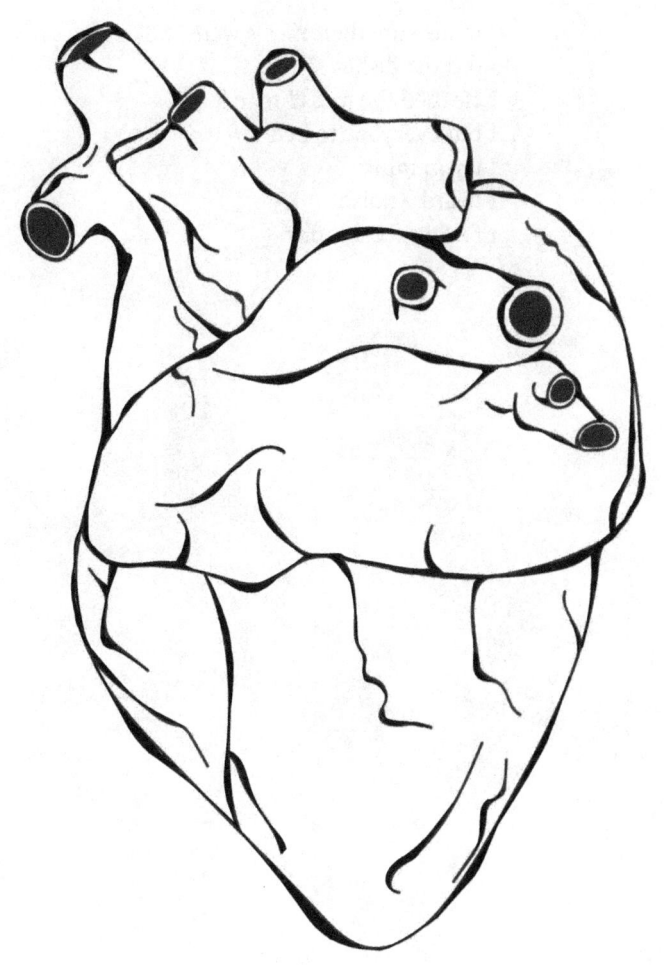

I made sure their meals were cooked
I did the dishes
I cleaned the mess I made
I put everyone to bed
I lay in mine
I heard a noise
I forgot to eat today

Let me know when
you have time to
grab a coffee

If I had time
I'd *grab* a shower

Mama Singh
How are you doing today
I turn around,
look at the nurse
Why are you calling
MY mother YOUR MAMA

You fell
I chose to watch
Stuck
My feet wouldn't move
You fell
I watched

There is nothing more
Than a mother's love
She wept, *We are older now*
I don't want to be old
I want my mother's love
Will I ever be too old
For a mother's love

My mind is racing
I do it all
Why am I doing it all
Why is no one helping me
She turned to me
You don't do enough
Will we ever
        do enough

She cries in pain
or is it fear
I try not to hear
I try not to cry
She turns to face
the other way
I turn on the fan,
whirring away
what I hope is
not real

I am sorry, Dad
I tried to hold you tight
He looks up at the doctor
She pushed me, that is how I fell

We all laugh

I tiptoe across the hall
swift and silent
worried he'll hear me
I open the door
and hush back
my socked feet sliding
across the wooden floor
I begin to shut my door
quietly, quietly
"Sonu," he calls from downstairs
my quiet was too loud

I study the new nurse
He knows the motions
He goes through them —
a robot in blue scrubs

Say something to him
Show him you care

He changes my father's shoes
and helps him to his feet

Talk to him
He can be unbroken
This will all go away

He walks my father
to the shower —
wordless, barely there

This is just a job to him
My father is just a job to him

I cry until my eyelids ache
Tears are wet but my eyes are dry
I can't close them
I want to sleep
If I sleep, I'll dream
I'll dream away this nightmare
    I need to sleep

I call to tell you she is sick
I call to tell you she is very, very sick
You tell me about your grandmother
How she died from her sickness
Monster! We are not talking about you!
She is not your grandmother
She is my mother
She is too young to die

She is not crying
    Why can't I be strong
Why am I crying
    When her eyes are dry
I pretend not to look at her
    But can she see
Why won't she cry
    I am older
I have more tears
    She is younger
She needs to live longer
    To have these tears

I pull away the curtain
Her skin is pink
Her breasts and stomach raw

If I don't look directly at her hand
I won't see the bones
Only her skin dripping
Like the wick of a candle

Where should I look

If I turn away will I hurt her

Why is everyone staring
Doctors, nurses, technicians
The whole burn unit burns
its eyes into my mother

Why can't someone
cover her body

Where are her clothes

He wipes tears from behind
his glasses, whispers
It's in God's Hands

Who is God
Why would He do this to us

I am crying
We are all crying

She is crying because
she wants to live

She asks out loud
*What kind of life have I lived
I haven't seen anything yet*

He wants to give her temples,
trips home, and most of all, time

He wants her to live
more than he wants
to keep his own life

God, he asks, *will you
let her live*

My heart is full of anger today

I want to say — *Can't you just walk*
Can't you just put your feet together and walk

I'm angry at his body for shutting down
I'm angry at him for not fighting harder

My anger is love

Get married in March, she murmurs

Her last wish — a spring wedding
for her oldest daughter

Seeing me married
will give her peace

She tells me she has no other worries
Only who will take care of me

I worry who will marry me
by March

Blood is thicker than water
    I am drowning
        Why won't someone save me
            Are they saving each other
                No one is listening
                    I need help
                        I need your help

Friends have stopped asking
I follow their pictures and posts
Their smiles seem brighter than usual
brighter and further away

I get the odd message

*How are you
How are your mom and dad*

Then nothing
for days

I want to say:
Your words
aren't enough

I want your shoes in my
front hall, your hands in
my hands, your lips on
my cheek

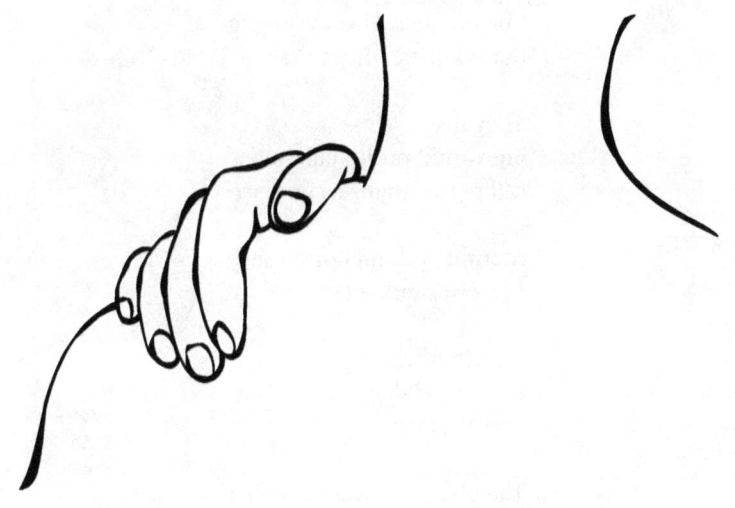

The phone is always ringing
but no one comes to call

They live so close
but would rather talk into a
cell phone than see our faces

Mouths spilling nonsense
Promises unkept

The doorbell rings —
more food delivered
by a stranger

The phone is always ringing
No one comes to call

Don't talk about it
If anyone asks
don't tell them
what really happened

Tell them she had an accident
Don't tell them everything

You know people and their
bad thoughts did this

Don't talk about it

Keep your thoughts to yourself

Then it never really happened

1:33 am
I threw Buddha's head on the wooden deck
White shattered ceramic glass
The smash was louder than the scream
I imagined would echo the dark streets
No one came out
Everything was broken to shattered glass

Forty — the worst year of my life

Your mother is dead
Mine is still alive

I beg you not to
compare them

I can still make memories
Yours will fade

Your mother is dead
Mine is still alive

What did I do

           to deserve this

She looks straight at him
curiosity hiding behind
dark glasses

I struggle to hold him up
He struggles to stand

Why do you keep looking
We feel your ugly eyes
He sees you
We see you

Stop looking

The sign reads *Burn Victim Survivors Christmas Party!!*
Some bits of tinsel, a Charlie Brown tree

Why are we celebrating pain
What happens to the ones who survive

Can they make new memories to erase
the painful ones from their past

My mom is leaving the hospital
but her scars will never fade

I walk back into the room
What happened, she asks
What did the doctor say

I turn away

She calls my name
as only a mother can

Why is she asking me
She can hear my tears
She can see my fear
She knows the answer

I turn to face her
my head in my hands

My tears are so loud
I can't hear anything

Don't come in here, I say
Leave us alone

All you do is tell us
your opinion

We have hope
We only have hope

You gave up on us
You gave up on our hope

Now leave us alone

He climbs back into the car
They look at each other
Best friends
I will see you soon, he says
They look again
They know
He holds his face
to gently say goodbye
Best friends who will
never see each other again

The shower is my quiet place
The water washes the silence
If I scrub hard enough
it can all be washed away
If I scrub hard enough
I can numb the pain

I hear a faint call
but pretend I don't
I linger in the steam
knowing they need me

I walk out and begin another day

I cannot rinse away sickness
I cannot quiet their needy noise
Their cries cut through the steam and glass
Their voices pry open a closed door

The tea is too hot
My tongue recoils

Coward!

She was lying in hot soup,
her body burnt

Who am I to complain

I gulp it down

I fix my gaze in the mirror
Give him privacy
His long shirt covers anything
a daughter shouldn't see
Up, I pull him up
I pull his pants up
My grip tight around his arm
My eyes locked in place
We do this each time
One day we won't even
be able to do this

Today he laughs
I help him up
He's having a good day
A memory plays in his eyes
My arms feel warm to him
He remembers a time we
both laughed

Like father
Like daughter

Have faith, she whimpers
She is crying in her sleep
I can hear her fear
when she tells me
*Hold your hands tightly
and pray*

You are both sick
I don't have enough hands

He lies in the next room
Not fighting anymore
      Not like her —
           She wants to live

His battle is done
We are still trying to win for him
      Should we also
      give up

What becomes of a man
When he is bedridden
      Will he be the dad
      or will I

Enjoy these last moments, they say
Smile
Be happy
You are spending time with them

Hypocrites!

You have no idea
What my time with them is like
How painfully the hands move

You have no idea how much I want
to rewind the clock

I hate time
My enemy
Sometimes I think I hate you

Should I ask for help
Should I ask you to come
I told you they are sick
You talk to me, but of
your silly problems
Why won't you see
what I am going through
Why won't you help

I take a sip

Oh, this feels good

We laugh
We eat

I smile
Guilty for my smiling
Guilty for all the drinking

I am having fun

So, how are your parents doing

The fun is over

I yell at my mommy today
because the house is too cold
This is her house
She always took care of us
She wakes from her nap,
walks downstairs slowly,
recovering her breath
on the way up

Even in her pain
she always puts me first

She will always be my Mommy

Today I have no words. Today only tears.

We are going in again today
Our second trip this week
They don't understand
You will wait for hours
under that bright light
It will make things worse for all of us
They'll tell us not to have hope
They'll tell us to give up
Everyone around us is sick
but still has hope

He slowly sits up
Out of breath
He asks, *why the both of us*
Why at the same time
I have no answer
I've always had the answers
Today I have none

She's fighting for life
Trying to win this losing battle
For the first time, I stand outside her door and
wonder if it would be easier for her to surrender

How much pain can she endure
How much can I witness

Why am I thinking these thoughts

Until she gives up
I won't give up
We will never give up

I am sorry, they all say,
one after another
Why is everyone sorry
You're sorry that they're alive
You'll apologize when they pass
You're sorry this happened to us
Do you know what you're sorry for
I am sorry

He turned around
and said *Thank you*
You're my daughter
My precious daughter
As if to tell me that I
meant the most to him
He didn't need to say it
I always knew
I will always know, Daddy

Why couldn't one of us be spared
Why the both of us

As if I had an answer

I looked away
That was my answer

How are you doing through all of this
Are you taking care of yourself

I tilt my head to show
a crooked part
flecked with grey

Have you seen these new arrivals
That's how much care I take

I pluck one strand
and present it

A gift
An accusation

Will you be at the wedding this weekend
I hear her muffled voice as she speaks to my
mother
I want to yell at her
You think she can go to a wedding
Why don't you come visit your sister
and help her come to that wedding
Or would you rather attend her
funeral

The phone rings again
Another person who can't be
bothered to come over
Why can't they drive here
No time to help take care of them, *me*
Why are they wasting my mother's last breaths
Why are they wasting our time
Why do they even call

My mother looks down
at her changed skin
A beauty queen
mourning her
ruined crown
I know my body
doesn't look good

It's almost an apology

Why is she giving up
I ignore her, point to
the book I bought online

It says we can change
everything around
The author is alive
He was sick like you
You can stay alive
Just believe in the
book of life

This place was already built for you
It could not have been altered
It was designed, and you
were pushed into one of its frames
Not a strong one, but
one with many holes
Now it's up to us to fill them
with love, before
cracks start to appear

Sometimes her pain gets so loud
we forget that he is sick, too

Did we sacrifice him
to save her

Did we spend all our prayers on her

Were there not enough to go around

We were so limited
I chose her

She loves opening gifts
He sits up and watches her
unravel the box
He smiles
What's in there
She lifts out a butter tart
She looks at him
There is only one

His eyes are shut to us
They look but cannot see
He no longer shares the stories
that used to fill our hearts

He is disappearing
I wish I could disappear too

Vomit dribbles down her chin
She has thrown up on herself again
What can I do to stop this
She rises slowly, thinking it's over, and
we walk to the car
Yet the sickness continues
I reach for a blanket
for my helpless mother
Her dried vomit sticks to her clothes

I am the child
Why am I seeing this

Her eyes are glittering
She's in a mood to share
Maybe my wish will come true
I lean in to catch her words
You'll meet a handsome doctor here
We hug, and her laugh lights
up the dark room

*You can't marry a man without
a car,* she says

We sit in the waiting room
This wait seems longer
There is more time to talk
More time for mother-daughter
matters

*Marry a man with many cars
One for me
One for you*

One day we will be orphans

We three will have no mother or father
They will leave us not by choice
They won't want to go
They won't want to abandon their children

We will still have each other
But we will never be fine without them

He's doing his dance again
One hand in the air
Even in a wheelchair
he's the life of this party
And she is smiling
She looks so beautiful
Who says they're ill
Tonight, they are
two parents enjoying
their youngest daughter's
wedding

This doctor is like all the others
She scorns our hope
She tells us it's not real
The only real is that they are sick
Have real, she says,
Don't have hope

He tells me I am
a lone soldier

That I have fallen
out of love

I tell him
All the love I have
belongs to them

There is nothing
left to share

He calls me a superhero
I call myself their child
Warrior

Who are you
I am Daddy's little girl
I think I say

Choose your favourite nursing home
I choose this home
I choose the home they built
To nurse them in
To nurse them home

I know this is difficult for you, he says
No
I know how much you have sacrificed
Nothing
I am sorry I did this to you
I am sorry I did this to you too

Pale in the colour of the sinking sun
Where has his body disappeared to
What has replaced it
Who is this man
I love someone I hardly know anymore
Where is my dad
His feet are sore

The more I drink, the more I cry
Friends offer to take me out for drinks
It's the only way to see anyone
It has been days since my last drink
Why do I continue to cry

I try to rinse away the fall
but the blood sticks
to his glasses
They are broken
just like him

He falls
We stay quiet
We struggle back up
No one talks about
what just befell us
We know it will happen again
We mouth the words
It will happen again
A lifeboat, a witness, a
hedge against surprise

Dad — your breakfast is ready
I balance his meal with a glass of milk
Shaky hands, steady walk

How's the food
Gross, he replies
I roll my eyes
Nothing will compare to his cooking

You're a good daughter
To be doing what
You are doing
Did I have a choice, I ask —
anger rising in my throat

Please ask me to marry you
I am being selfish
Both of my sisters have
someone to take care of them
after we become orphans
Will you take care of me
I may not be in love with you
Please marry me so I won't
be alone when they pass
Please don't leave me alone

Last year I laughed more
than I cried
Last year I was happy
Why can't I remember last year

No one comes to visit
They forget the days we had planned
No one seems to remember
the story I shared
Did you just forget to care

Where do my prayers go
If I get closer to your
image, will you hear my
fear, see how tightly my
hands are clasped

I believe you are real
I believe you have the
power to help

Must I choose one
or can I choose both

I move away from your image
Five years, I plead
I promise to be good
for five years

She whispers in my ear
Come with me
I follow her along
empty halls to a
cold waiting room
I leave my jacket on
to protect myself
to shield my heart
She leans in
I lean out
I am a patient, too
I am sick and
confused
You're a doctor
She holds my hand
You are strong
Why is she glowing
Why is her skin so pale
You will always be strong
She stands
I follow
She leaves
I will never see
my angel again

I swing open the gate
and it's already too late
I have lost control
Now I am screaming at
my baby sister and she is
screaming back
What are we even saying
Our words are riderless horses
Control has left the track

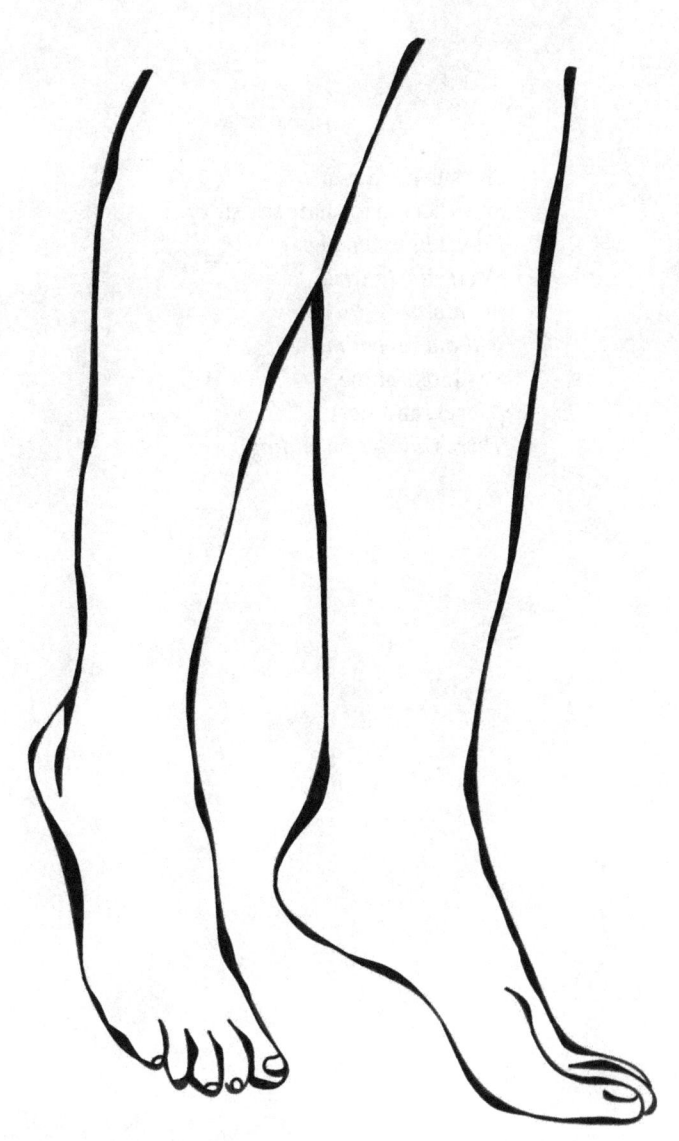

She sits me down
She asks me to share my story
I don't have one, I say
I'm trying to write
my mother's story
without an ending
She looks at me,
pauses, and says
There's always an ending

I'm crying so hard my body shakes
The words can't be understood
Why am I calling anyone
Why am I crying
Why is this happening

This crying
        calling
                shaking

Is this all I am now

Soaked in water
Trying to escape through the shower drain
I'm pushing down with my feet
Go down
Why won't you go down
It's too thick
It's too much
My hair won't wash down the drain
Oh, I am losing my hair

You're not my friend
I told you my secret
I shared my fears
You watched my fears multiply
and when I left, you
never came to get me

This cape is getting tight
Breathing is hard
Hope has taken flight
I'm smaller now, less able to leap
My thoughts match the darkness
I just want to sleep

Cold bare halls
Muffled cries for help
Someone asks for water
Someone is sobbing
I'll walk fast
I can't help
I can only walk past
in silence
like they do

Are you about to sneeze, she laughs
Your mouth is open
She plugs away on the computer
Takes my mom's temperature

No
I am about to have a panic attack

Do rocks ever become tired
They say I'm a rock
Rocks can't feel how tired they are
I'm so tired

The sun wakes me up
Warms my numb heart
I pray
I meditate
I am grateful
Today will be a great day

The reports come in
Today is the worst day
I look around this sterile space
I am shoved, hearing sounds
Noises distract me from the doctor's words
Why are you telling me this here
Couldn't you pick a better time or
place — like nowhere and never

Daddy, she is really sick today
He looks at me, terrified
His body trembles
Tears stream down his face
He looks around the room
His three daughters
His wife asleep upstairs
Who will take care of me, he asks

We sisters sit around my bed
We share stories about her
We are laughing and smiling
I wipe this joy off my face
It feels wrong to laugh and smile
when she is lying in the other room
so close to death

Stop this, I say
Leave my room

Mom, Mom, Mommy
I'm yelling now
    MOM!
Light from her bedroom door
streams across her face
MOM, are you awake
MOM, wake up —

I'm OK, she says,
then turns and
goes back to sleep
I sigh in disbelief
Tonight she is still alive
Tonight we're being
given a little more time

My grandmother enters the room
hunched over in heartache
She stands near her son-in-law as he weeps
She holds his head in her hands
Does she ever wish it was him
instead of her oldest daughter

For a few minutes after she wakes,
our mom is all brisk efficiency

Make sure you check the mail often
Pay the property tax on time
Your father — take care of him
Sell our house
Don't fight with your sisters
Donate the money in my drawers
to those less fortunate
Give away the clothes I have never worn
to people in need

Her voice winds down
She needs sleep

All I want is an end to these words
and for both of them to live forever

Dad, you have to eat something
My heart is empty
I cannot eat
Please, Dad, look — she is eating
Take one bite
He looks at her, then looks away from me
Forty-three years I have spent with her
Now you have taken my right arm

My friend stands before me, saying words
I hope this never happens to my parents
You think I wanted this to happen to mine
Do you think I asked for this
What kind of friend are you
The words you say make me feel worse
Can't you make me feel better, for once

Who have I become
Uneven lines across this beautiful face
Dark spots and cracked skin
They weren't there before
Eyes open, too tired to shut
Unwashed hair
A faint smell

I am a caregiver
who has forgotten
to care for herself

While driving,
I miss my exit

It's too late to turn back
I'll drive until I reach the next one
I wonder, Can they sail past death
the way I sailed past this turnoff

You must stop crying
I hold the phone away
I try to hide my sadness
You have cried enough
Tears won't change anything
If she isn't crying
neither should you
My mouth is dry
He continues to talk
You are the oldest daughter
Be brave — show everyone
how strong you are

It's a curse, they whisper
The whole family is cursed
Both parents sick
Oldest daughter unmarried
Someone has put a curse on them
The curse made everyone sick
Let's leave
before it spreads to us

Take off your shoes
Cover your head
Walk to the front
Don't look at anyone
Listen to words you will never understand
Hug everyone in the front row
Walk down the middle
Sit in an empty seat
Listen to more words you don't understand
His body will be cremated
I leave because I understand that

How many gods can I pray to
If I pray in English will the Indian gods understand
Who will hear me if I pray in Punjabi
Is anyone listening who can keep them alive
My pen breaks
No one is listening now

She asks me to make her favourite food
Don't tell your sisters I cheated
It's our secret
We look at him
He shakes his head and smiles
I want some too
He reaches for an Indian dessert
We eat our secret in silence

www.ingramcontent.com/pod-product-compliance
Lightning Source LLC
LaVergne TN
LVHW041545070426
835507LV00011B/941